The Church in
Transition

The Church in Transition

Three Talks on Bowen Family Systems Theory and Dealing with Change in the Church

Ronald W. Richardson

Ronald W. Richardson, Tucson, Arizona. Published 2017.
© 2017 Ronald W. Richardson

ISBN-13: 978-1547080175
ISBN-10: 1547080175
Interior illustration on page 10: Amy Haagsma

Table of Contents

Preface

A note to the reader about this book's style. I have done a simple transformation of my verbally presented workshops to manuscript form. To keep expenses down, I did not hire a professional editor, and I have not done much in the way of editing the book myself. The talks are as I gave them without much alteration. I present them to you in an extremely casual format, leaving in many of my usual writing mistakes; I hope this does not get in the way of your understanding the material. The parts in **bold print** were on my PowerPoint slides for the talks.

Ron Richardson
ronwrichardson.com

Introduction

Becoming Your Best in Transition

We have all been in transit from the time of our birth. Life is one transition after another as we move from one way or form of life to another. There are a number of normal life cycle transitions that all individuals and families go through as they have children and raise them. Churches also go through certain predictable life cycle transitions as they grow and shrink and change. Sometimes, these changes goes smoothly, but at other times they can be very difficult and upsetting for those involved.

I gave the three lectures in this little book on the occasion of a Lutheran Synod dealing with the retirement of one bishop and the installation of a new one. Everyone involved knew there would be transition issues related to this change. They invited me to speak on transitions from a Bowen family systems theory perspective. That is the substance of this short book.

Bowen family systems theory offers concrete ideas around how to understand what makes transitions difficult and how to go through them in ways that are productive for all involved. In these lectures, I address specific examples in our own lives. I also relate how Bowen theory illuminates a significant transition in the life of the early church as described in the Book of Acts and in Galatians. The three talks are titled:

1. How Normal Transitions Become Difficult: Anxiety and Emotional Systems (Acts 10:1–48)
2. Going from Bad to Worse in Transitions and How to Avoid This: Triangles and Detriangling (Acts 11:2, 13:45, 15:2 and 5, and Galatians)
3. Making even Difficult Transitions Work Better: Differentiation of Self (Acts 15:8–10, Galatians 2:11–14)

Chapter 1

How Normal Transitions Become Difficult:

Anxiety and Emotional Systems

(Acts 10:1–48)

Anxiety and emotional systems

It is an honor to be here with you in the Synod on this important occasion. Thank you for the invitation. I hope I am able to add something useful for your consideration as you undergo the changes this event will bring.

Most of you know the name of Milton Friedman, the very conservative economist who was a hero of Barry Goldwater's (also among some contemporary politicians) known for his acerbic comments like, "There are no free lunches." Once a colleague of his took him out to lunch and paid for it, and then said to Friedman, "You see Milton, there are free lunches." To which Friedman replied, "Oh no, this was not a free lunch. I had to listen to you for two hours." Well, you folks have me for over three hours of listening and the Synod is paying for my lunch.

I have been asked to speak about transitions in the church context. I don't suppose there was any particular transition in mind when this was suggested! Life cycle transitions are not just about individuals, they are also about systems that are undergoing change. Loren Mead's classic book, *A Change of Pastors*, tends to focus more on the individual aspects of transitions, but I want to look at the larger social context, from the point of view of family systems theory.

We are all highly experienced at doing transitions. We are not neophytes. Like it or not, life is about constantly being in transition in one way of living to another. Some transitions we welcome eagerly and some we fear or dread. One *New Yorker* cartoon shows the robed figure of Death leading a man out of the door of his house. His wife is saying to him as he leaves "Don't worry, dear. Change is good."

We know about the major life cycle transitions in families. I won't go through them all but here is a short list:

Leaving home as young adults, getting married, having children, perhaps divorcing and remarrying, even having more children, launching our children, advancing through careers, perhaps changing careers, becoming grandparents, retiring, losing a partner through illness and death, and finally transiting out of life ourselves.

All of these involve whole systems, not just individual people. Each one involves emotional as well as practical challenges for the people involved. Churches also go through certain predictable transitions as they grow and shrink and change over time, and they also involve challenges. We church leaders transit through various official positions and assignments. In addition, over time, we change theologically and develop spiritually. We accept new positions and take on new responsibilities. Sometimes we are demoted from them.

As you have now installed a new Bishop, we remember the words once used during papal coronations: **"Sic transit gloria mundi."** They are usually translated as "Thus passes the glory of the world." The words are meant to remind us of the transitory nature of life itself and that whatever status we may have achieved, like being a Bishop, or even a Pope, it also will pass. They remind us to be humble, not to cling too tightly to that status, and to remember that we will all end up in the same place when life itself comes to an end. Whatever is, will not last and something new will come. We all need to be ready to "transit."

Our denominations have even developed a new specialized ministry called **Interim Ministry**. These short-term ministers focus on helping congregations make good transitions as they get ready to call new leadership, or as a new way of organizing their life as a community. They help congregations deal with the difficult issues left over from past ministries that have not been resolved, and to plan for the future ministry of the church. Sometimes, too much is expected of these Interims. Another cartoon has a church member on the Pastoral Search Committee speaking with an Interim Minister. The church member says, "As an interim minister you'll be expected to clean up the situation which has been developing for years. How many weeks do you think it will take?"

The words we use to describe transitions are usually nouns that denote a specific event, like retirement. In fact, all transitions are processes. We need to think in terms of transitive verbs. They are about movement and change that take place over time. In addition, our process of being in transit is not just about us individually as the only subject; it is also about all of those connected with us, and their reactions to our movement in life. This is true here in this Synod.

Transitions can be difficult and challenging. Even those we welcome and look forward to, like promotions, are not always easy and may bring unwanted surprises. We have all probably made some good transitions and perhaps some we have done poorly. I know I have. Looking back at my own life and career, there are some I have done very poorly.

Our pastoral care ministry with church members most often occurs around their transitions in life. We all want to be at our best in dealing with our transitions but often we cannot. In these three talks, I will attempt to clarify what makes them difficult and how we can be at our best as we transit through life, looking at them from the point of view of Bowen family systems theory. The theory offers specific concepts around how to understand what makes transitions difficult and how to go through them in ways that are productive for all involved.

Transitions in the Book of Acts

I love the Book of Acts. One reason is simply because it shows us that the early church had problems not unlike our own. In the very beginnings of our church, those early Jews who had come to accept Jesus as the Messiah struggled to clarify the meaning of the truly major transition they were going through. They went from the glory of experiencing the resurrection, and the ascension of Jesus, and the gift of the Holy Spirit, to angrily fighting among themselves. They had conflicts over who their legitimate leaders were, and having major theological differences that split their ranks. These early issues nearly sank this young movement before it really got off the ground.

Toward the end of Chapter 9 in Acts, Luke writes, "So the church throughout all Judea and Galilee and Samaria had peace and was built up . . . ." The end? No, of course that was not the end of the story. It was a brief respite. We can never count on peace remaining. That peace was going to be disturbed big time. Beginning in the next chapter and through the rest of Acts, the church was going to be somewhat preoccupied with several significant transitions.

Chapter 10 tells us about the beginning of a major shift in the Jesus movement. You remember it well. It is about the inclusion of gentiles into the promises of God. It is about the Roman Centurion Cornelius becoming a believer. Up to this point, Christianity was primarily a movement within Judaism for Jews and it was called "The Way."

Peter led this change due to a vision he had while praying. Indeed, he had this vision three times before he became convinced. It challenged his most basic Jewish beliefs. God gave him an image of all of the animals of the world being lowered down to him in a sheet and God told him he could freely eat of them. Peter protested that he could not eat anything unclean and God said, **"Do not call common what God has cleansed. Rise Peter, kill, and eat."** This was a revolutionary idea. Peter had no idea at the time as to what would eventually come of this change. It also indicates, if I wanted to get a good fight started right not, that God was not a vegetarian. But I won't get into my low-carb beliefs right now!

Anyway, the next day Peter goes and meets Cornelius, and his household, and Peter says to them, **"You know how unlawful it is for a Jew to associate with or to visit anyone of another nation; but God has shown me that I should not call any man common or unclean . . . . Truly I perceive that God shows no partiality but in every nation anyone who fears him and does what is right is acceptable to him."** And the Jews who accompanied Peter were amazed at what he said and did.

Word of him doing this spread quickly through the ranks of believers. They said, "Do you know what Peter has done? He has associated with gentiles, and not only that, he has eaten their food. He has had table fellowship with them." The other leaders of the movement at that time questioned Peter about what he had done and, after he explained, they went along with him and agreed that the good news of Jesus Christ must include the gentiles, those previously excluded from the Jewish faith. Then, beginning with

Chapter 11, Luke tells how things really began to change through Paul's ministry to the gentile world.

The systemic interconnected change process

As I said, **transitions are more about verbs than nouns. They are about movement and change. In addition, they are interactive.** They are about groups of closely related people. Our process of being in transit is not just about each one of us individually as the only subject; it is also about all of those connected with us, and their reactions to our movement in life, and our reactions to their reactions to our movement, and of course their own movement in life also affects us, etc. We all have emotional issues connected with these changes. Just like in the Jerusalem church, we react to those leading the change and they react to our reactions. This is part of what is called **emotional process within an emotional system**.

I like to use the image of a hanging mobile (see next page) when talking about systems.

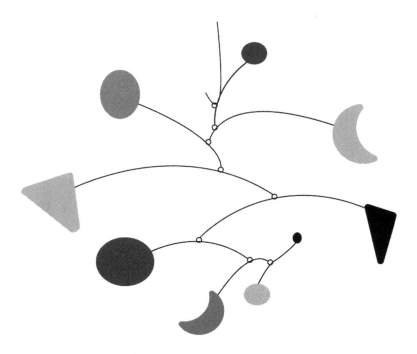

We are each pieces in a mobile, connected to one another in a delicate emotional balance, and as one of us changes our position in the mobile, all of the other pieces are affected. I used to make mobiles, and it is a delicate business. The balance of the whole will be off kilter as one or more pieces move closer in to the center of gravity, or further out. If one piece disappears, or another piece is added, all of the other pieces have to adjust. All of a sudden, because of some movement over there, with other people, we ourselves are spinning and bouncing up and down.

In addition, (and this is a little difficult to show graphically) we are each pieces in a number of interconnected mobiles (like the family mobile, the church mobile, our work mobile, with our friends and social groups, our communities, etc.) and as shifts occur in any one of these, the other mobiles are also affected. First, Peter's personal system of beliefs was challenged, this spreads to his immediate associates, to Cornelius and his family, and then to the leadership in Jerusalem. Even the mission of the church in the world was affected.

This interconnectedness of life is deeper and more powerful than we usually like to believe. None of us are truly independent operators. The event of installing a new bishop is an on-going process that has involved changes and shifts in the mobile up until now that long preceded the specific installation event of last night, and there will be many more shifts to come. We will each have our reactions to this event that will be part of an ongoing process. We will have adjustments to make. Although we will all be looking for balance, for homeostasis and the peace of Acts 9, there will be some unbalancing for everyone involved. We can count on this story continuing in Acts 10. This is the way it is in human community.

Anxiety

The one element that all transitions, good and bad, have in common is anxiety. If we get a promotion, we can feel anxious; if we get fired, we can feel anxious. That anxiety is the sense of threat that underlies our uncertainty about what is to come, or our predictions about what will come. The early church in Acts 10 was highly anxious about the change that was happening and the implications of this revolutionary shift. What would it mean for them if they gave up a central Jewish practice and belief they had followed for centuries? Where would it lead if they started having table fellowship with gentiles, and even welcomed them into their faith? There is an implied threat to their whole way of life.

From our own perspective here today, we think of the shift back then as a natural, good thing. We say, "Why of course it was the correct thing to do. What's the big deal?" But at the time, it looked horrifying to some people in this young movement. Many Jewish believers were greatly disturbed and uncertain about this major departure in their beliefs. Just think about it. All their lives they had lived out their beliefs in a certain way that had governed every action. This distinction between them and the gentiles was a central critical issue in their faith and now it is called into question. They didn't just make up these rules. They were God-given rules for living a clean, pious, and righteous life.

Bowen theory defines anxiety as the experience of threat, real or imagined. The threat is anything that upsets the balance of the mobile, any shift of one of the parts in a system creates uncertainty and the possibility of threat in the other parts.

Anxiety is an instinctive response when the homeostasis in our mobile has been upset. Change is the wind that blows through our various mobiles and we react with "Hold on! What is going on here? We have to do something to calm things down." Bowen recognized that this is not just an individual phenomenon. He understood that organizations like the church are not just a collection of individual people. The church is, in itself, a living system and anxiety can run through it just as it does when an individual or a family experiences some kind of shock.

The early church was in turmoil around this new understanding of what their faith meant. No question that their old ways of practicing their faith was undergoing dramatic change. Their mobile was swinging around wildly. It must have seemed chaotic and individual members did not know what to believe or who to follow.

To be in a church, just like to be in a family, is to have to deal with recurring experiences of anxiety. The only non-anxious church is a dead church. That church is not living and moving and growing. We can count on the fact that we will move on from the end of Acts 9 to Acts 10, from peace to major disturbance. Even the last chapter of Acts was not the end of this tumultuous church story, not by a long ways. To be alive is to have to experience and deal with anxiety. This is almost always in the form of some challenge or change, some transition. Even if we ourselves think we are not experiencing anxiety, we almost certainly are in relationship with people who are anxious through the complex system of interactions in our mobile so that even people we may not know, or are not close to, are affecting us.

From time to time through its history, the church itself experiences threat and is under attack from outside its walls. At those times, all the members and leaders normally join together to fight against the attack, just like a family does. We fuse together to resist the attack; we are indeed at our most cooperative time with one another. Afterward we say, "Well that crisis made us stronger." We feel good about belonging to one another.

However, when things are calmer externally, then internally, within the church. We start paying more attention to our differences. We can begin to perceive each other as a threat, to ourselves individually or to the community of believers. For example, someone might want to get us fired from our position, or replace us as the head of a committee, or the threat could be to our own version of what we believe the church should be, or to what we believe theologically. I will not go through the catalogue of threats facing the church today. You know them—the list is hugely extensive, from major to minor, and you all have your own examples that you are dealing with right now.

We are in a time when major church groups are separating from one another, leaving denominational structures that have been dear to them. Those leaving have felt under attack from others in the denomination and ultimately they decide they have to leave and form their own denomination. When they have done so, they feel good. They celebrate and have joy in their movement.

But afterward, as time passes, little things begin to happen within the new denomination or congregation; these separated groups begin to think that some in their movement are not as committed to the principles they separated for, and that a further refinement of beliefs needs to happen. They become irritated with one another. They argue and begin to attack one another. Ultimately, down the road, they may decide another separation is in order from those who didn't really get what it was all about.

These internal threats can be the most insidious, the most challenging, and the most difficult even to talk about. This is what I was dealing with in my marriage and family therapy clinical practice all of the time. Sometimes we don't, or we can't talk about these challenging issues without losing our cool and so, just like a married couple, we shut up, we stew and simmer, and then we start thinking divorce. We say to ourselves, "I can't stand this person. I have got to get out of this marriage." Most of the couples I saw were thinking this way when I started counseling with them.

These internal threats in the church can fester and simmer. Calling them something like "church politics" makes it too superficial. Members of the church pit themselves against each other and they feel separate from each other. The members begin to divide into camps. You know who your enemies are, and they may perceive you as their enemy. This can all come to a head during times of transition, when some major issue, that defines the nature of what we think the church should be, comes out into the open and a battle is joined. But a long process has lead up to this point and there will be ongoing fallout in the system after "the event" is over, all related to the experience of anxiety.

The anxiety is contagious; it spreads through the membership, even when people don't really know what is going on. They can be totally uninformed as to the nature of the battle but they are anxious, like a herd of wild animals that bolts when one member of the group thinks it has seen a predator, reacts, and starts running. Soon the whole herd is running. If they had such consciousness, one animal could say to the other, "What are we running from?" and the other would say, "I don't know, I didn't see anything, but it must be serious because our leader is running."

As humans, we are much more nuanced than wild animals and the threat does not have to be as concrete as an encounter with a predator. If one of us is just very uncomfortable with a situation or a development in the church, and if that person holds any kind of a position of influence, they can communicate the discomfort to others. They can ascribe any number of reasons for it, and maybe tell others, and they will be uncomfortable because that one person is. It is difficult sometimes to pinpoint the nature of the anxiety, but that doesn't keep us from having it, and reacting to it.

In these kinds of situations, we can do dumb things. When someone else moves in the emotional mobile and the balance is upset. We may then move to try to rebalance the system but our movement only adds to the unbalancing. Others then, naturally become anxious and they move in an effort to rebalance and the unbalancing gets worse, like when somebody incorrectly tries to rebalance a rocking rowboat.

We react instinctively to the unbalancing, reactivity leads to reactivity, but we don't think about what is going on, we may not see the big picture, and what is going to result from our efforts. For humans, when the perceived threat is not actually life threatening, but we treat it as if it is, our instinctive reactions often get us into deeper trouble. Things begin to snowball and we get results we did not really intend originally.

Here are just a few signs of anxiety running our emotional system:

- **People dividing into camps automatically, based on emotional reactions, rather than clearly thinking through their own beliefs and positions.**

- People fighting over turf or territory, and sneaky political moves or backstabbing.
- People having major emotional arguments, attacking others and defending self.
- Blaming and scapegoating others, name calling, and ad hominem arguments that negatively characterize the opponents, their personalities, and their motivations.
- People justifying their own behavior saying that, "The reason I am acting this way is because of the way he is behaving. I wouldn't do what I am doing if he wasn't doing what he is doing." We think someone else is causing our behavior.
- People doing "end runs" around the official policies and procedures of the church, not acting in accord with the organizational or hierarchical practices.
- People simply working harder, more zealously, on the immediate issue rather than stepping back and being able to think, saying, "Wait a minute, what is going on here?"
- Failure to perform one's duties and be responsible, to be distracted, to overlook important details, or do needed follow-up on things agreed to.
- Vague, conflicting, and mixed messages from the leadership.
- Failed initiatives that go nowhere.

- **Greater distance between those who are at odds with each other, or people going quiet, refusing to engage, hiding out in an office or failing to come to a meeting or to church worship.**
- **Total obstructionism and refusal to budge or negotiate anything.**
- **People capitulating and going along with a decision just to "keep the peace."**
- **Turnover of people in particular positions.**
- **People getting sick, physically or emotionally, so that they cannot follow through on their once heavy involvement.**

The list could go on. There are so many signs of anxiety in a system. We sometimes call it stress but the two are not the same. In fact, anxiety is our response to stress. Different people can be more or less anxious about the same stressor in the system.

The anxiety leads to endless feedback loops and spreads in the organization. Very often, one person, or one group of people get fingered as the "bad guys" and they are focused on as "disturbers of the peace." Almost never does this have a good outcome. The "bad guys" can even be fired, but the emotional process will continue with those still in the system.

I am not saying that there is no such thing as people with psychological issues or ways of problematic functioning that create difficulties. Such individual people do exist. But when a system is less anxious, and the people in it can be more thoughtful, they can do a good job of relating to these people, not getting anxious, and getting on with their mission. **When a system is anxious, it is easy to focus our anxiety on one individual or one group of people and see them as the problematic ones, and scapegoat them.**

The brain and anxiety

Our brains are wired just like the rest of the animal world to react quickly to threat. When threatened, our brain automatically releases several hormones designed to lead to certain behavioral responses commonly known as the fight/flight reaction.

Actually, the whole range of reactions to the sense of threat is **freeze, flee, fight, and faint**. Each of these behaviors can be life saving, and they are automatic. That is good. If we had to stop and think about what to do when a speeding car is about to hit us, we would likely die. We react because our brain is designed to bypass our slower and more thoughtful cerebral cortex and go straight from our senses to the hypothalamus and the amygdala, then immediately to our muscles and without thinking, we jump out of the way. It is automatic, thank God. Afterward, the flood of hormones in our body can make us feel sick or shaky.

The problem, of course, is that we can react the same way to things that are only perceived threats, not real threats like being hit by a speeding car, where we will actually die. If I have survived a flood but lost everything else, it could happen, with enough anxiety, that I will begin to think every rainstorm is going to bring another flood. This is an imagined threat. There is no imminent flood, but we react as if there is. As long as we keep imagining a threat, our bodies will react as if it is really there, and respond accordingly. We will be worried, tense, and "feel stressed."

I have one more *New Yorker* cartoon. She is standing in the doorway from the kitchen to the living room with her hands on her hips and an angry look on her face. She has a T-shirt on that says, "Fight." He is sitting in his living room chair with a timid, fearful look on his face, and his T-shirt says, "Flight." In any emotional system, we can have people who represent one or the other stance. Things can remain this way in the system for long periods of time with no change taking place—only people feel more and more worn down by it all.

The typical kind of contemporary reactions we have in anxious situations are somewhat modified from the reptilian responses of fight/flight. They are only a bit more nuanced but still we have the same kind of automatic reactions. They are:

1. **We comply or keep the peace, go along with what is expected and don't rock the boat. This is equivalent to "freeze."**
2. **We run away or distance, physically or emotionally. This refusal to face an issue is "flight."**
3. **We engage in open conflict and wage war on each other. This is "fight."**
4. **We develop physical, emotional, or social disability in one or more key system members. This is a kind of "faint."**

One strategy related to #1 above is to get others to become "team players." We push for unity and discourage disagreement. Very often this means doing things the way the person or group in charge wants them done. One other image we like to use is "we are a family." This will often mean we do it the way dad wants, or how mom wants things to be. In both of these, "togetherness as sameness" is considered the most important value. Anxiety tends to provoke togetherness as sameness. It says that we all have to think and feel and act as if we are one person.

Perhaps you know of a time when that has happened in a group. Team-building retreats or exercises are fine when they involve getting to know one another better. If they involve trying to "get us all on the same wavelength," they can be a disaster. If people are persuaded to stop thinking for self, if they are encouraged to fuse together into an oneness in belief and action, then they may coalesce around the least provocative members of the group and many members then dumb themselves down. They shut down their intelligence, their beliefs, and they go along to get along.

One very important aspect of anxiety-based thinking is that it emphasizes unity. We should all think and feel the same way. It is not comfortable with diversity. Of course, in real-life threatening situations, unity is essential. That is why the military is organized the way it is. That is when hierarchy works the best, but even then the military has always profited from diversity—people from different kinds of backgrounds with different perspectives applied to the common task. However, the military also requires innovative thinkers, people with imagination and individuality. Often these people become war heroes who go beyond the call of duty.

Let me be clear. I am not one who argues for consensus in thinking and feeling before taking action. The great moments of change in human history, the most important transitions, did not rely on consensus. Usually they involved an individual who was willing to step out in a new direction and take the risk of disapproval or failure. The consensus follows later.

Coming down to the level I have the most experience with, change happens this way in couples and family therapy. When one member of the family says, "Okay, I have thought this through for myself and this is what I am going to do." That person automatically becomes the leader in the family for that period of time. Their action challenges others in the family to start thinking and acting out of their own individuality as well.

One example. I worked with a family of four adult siblings and their mother. The siblings all had their own families. Father had died two years earlier. Major transitions were going on in this family in addition to their grief. However, father had been the emotional kingpin; things revolved around him and his wants. Mom, who had been his supporter, was somewhat at a loss because of his death but she was starting to move on in her life. The family came to see me in part because they were at odds around how to handle one legacy from dad. They each co-owned a large ski chalet. The land was bought, and built on by dad along with all of the family members. It was an extremely large house that all the families, with children, could stay in at the same time and do things together. This had been dad's dream of how to keep the family together and mom had helped to promote it.

I will simplify the story by saying they experienced a number of conflicts around the use and management of this property. Many chores needed doing to maintain it. Each of the adult children also had careers and families of their own. It required a huge amount of time. Some members thought they should sell the property, and some thought they should "all pitch in and make it a real family place just like dad wanted." One person said, "It is a way to remember dad and keep his presence among us." Mom tended to be in this camp. This togetherness orientation kept them in conflict and the leaders of this group tried to guilt the others into being more involved and more caring (like saying "Don't you want us to be a family together like dad wanted?"). They wanted me to help them come to an agreement around how to unite around dealing with the property.

In the process of talking it through and finding out what the chalet meant to each one of them, after a number of sessions, the oldest son who was the most responsible in many ways, said to the group, "My wife and I have decided to pull out of any involvement in this property. We will continue to pay our fair share of the financial costs for those who want to maintain it, but we are going our own way with regard to working on the chalet and the land itself." There was a major negative reaction at first. There was lots of anger and accusations of betrayal and of not caring, being selfish, destroying the family togetherness, etc. But the oldest son maintained his position.

After a few more family group sessions, the mood changed. There was a general feeling of relief in the family and a sense that others also felt freer to have a life of their own rather than trying to live some kind of fantasy of what a family "should be" and what "dad would want." They decided they did not need the property to keep the memory of dad alive or to keep mom happy and not feeling so alone. They worked out a deal with regard to the property that would allow the son who was most invested in it and had a vision for it to be the person in charge, and it was his responsibility with the others having financial shares to help pay the costs. They each got on more freely and happily with their own lives in their own families. In addition, their sense of their own larger family improved.

This change took one person to have the courage to step out from the family emotional togetherness on his own and, as the unofficial leader of the family, to take a difficult stand that he knew would bring grief down on him. Crucially, he was able to stay related to each of them, not withdraw, or defend, or attack, or crumble, but to stay interested in their thoughts and reactions and still insist on the direction that made sense to him.

In Bowen theory, what he did is called differentiation of self. I will say more about that in each of the remaining sessions. The point here is that there is nearly always a way to stay connected with one another that does not require that members have to give up self and conform. This is the way that groups most often make headway through the difficult transitions they face. Someone takes a better-differentiated stand. There is often a time of reaction and perhaps group chaos, and greater anxiety. But eventually, if the group leader can maintain the stand, non-reactively, and keep emotional contact with the rest of the group, then the group mobile of the emotional system begins to rebalance and stabilize, often in a more comfortable and enjoyable way.

Two kinds of thinking

As human beings, we have a cerebral cortex, the outer part of our brain that allows greater rationality and objectivity. It helps us solve difficult problems, live more effectively, and be happier. It is capable of abstract thinking and planning, and it can interrupt or undercut the automatic reactions of the older part of our brain that some have called the reptilian brain. We can use this part of our brain to evaluate what is really a threat and what is not actually threatening. To do this, we have to think things through.

Just about every book I read nowadays refers to Daniel Kahneman's book *Thinking, Fast and Slow*. Kahneman is a Nobel Prize–winning psychologist but the award was in the field of economics. He is the leader of what is now called behavioral economics. **Much like Bowen theory, he is interested in what people actually do when dealing with questions of value, not what the traditional economic theories say they should do rationally.** It may be a surprise that traditional economists did not realize people do not behave rationally or in their best interest economically. They react with their gut rather than with their thinking brain. Kahneman calls the gut reactions fast thinking. We sometimes call it intuitive thinking. Sometimes that way of thinking is bang-on, but much of the time it is critically wrong.

Much of our thinking is guided by our anxiety and often we are not aware that this is happening. **Anxiety-based thinking can be very clever, very deep, and very intelligent, but it can also be based on the false prem-**

ise that there is a real threat facing us. Anxiety-based thinking is automatic, and it is quick. We take little time for reflection. It usually does not inspire us to say to ourselves, "Wait a minute. I am reacting right now out of my anxiety." It simply accepts the anxiety and runs with it. It is also called "knee-jerk thinking." The usual goal of this kind of thinking is to reduce our level of anxiety. **It is also called "quick fix" thinking, meaning do what it takes to fix the anxiety, not the situation that led to it.**

Within the social context of the church, we can usually tell if it is anxiety-based thinking if what we are thinking about is focused on others and how we will "get them," or change them, or win them over, or defeat them, or humiliate them, or get rid of them in our lives. To the extent we do other-focused thinking, we are continuing the reactive process. They may well be thinking the same way about us and it will be an on-going process of tit for tat. If our solution to our anxiety is to get someone else to change in some way, we are doomed to on-going reactivity and ultimate failure.

Thinking that is much more useful in anxious situations is focused on self and self's own behavior; "What will I or won't I do in this situation?" It involves taking responsibility only for self. Bowen theory also calls this more differentiated stance taking an "I-position." It involves thinking through our own beliefs and principles for how we want to behave with others and then following through in our actions. This usually slower, self-focused thinking leads us to think about something we can actually do something about which is our own actions. That is what the older brother did in the family I mentioned above.

He stopped trying to convince other family members about what they should do, and just took responsibility for himself. Rather than trying to change others, and experiencing the frustrations of that effort, we can simply decide how we will be in any given situation. This is normally when we do our best thinking. Then we can clearly communicate to others who we are, what we will and will not do, and what they can expect of us.

In slow thinking, we have to become aware first of our automatic, anxiety-driven thinking and reactions. We may sound very calm, cool, collected, and judicious in what we verbalize and how we argue or discuss an issue with others but in fact it can still be our emotionality that is running us. Many rational-sounding partners (usually husbands) I have worked with in my practice attempted to use reason over against the more overt emotionality of their partner. However, underneath their rationality, they were just as emotionally reactive, and experiencing just as much threat, as were their partners. They didn't know they were anxious, and being emotionally reactive in their use of rationality. Both partners have to find a more thoughtful way of being present with each other in the marriage when facing anxiety-provoking situations.

The things we get anxious about in our relationships, and our typical reactive patterns for dealing with it, normally go back to our experience in our family of origin. We developed our automatic patterns there, while growing up. When stressful stuff started to come our way then, and we then felt some degree of threat, we began more and more to rely on these old patterned ways of coping.

Contemporary neuroscience has shown exactly how we maintain our reactive patterns over the years. **Those sensitivities we have to the actions of others, that stimulate our own anxiety and our reactive patterns, are very deeply ingrained and not easy to change. But they are not impossible to change.** Going back into one's family of origin and working on changing self (not them) in that context is one of the best ways to develop a stronger self. The older brother in my example had to let go of his patterned way of thinking about responsibility.

Any move we can make in this direction, of reflecting on our own actions and what we will or won't do, will have an automatic effect in our church lives of slowing down and calming down the reactive process. Note the point here: **we do not engage in the normal and quite reactive action focused on others or trying to calm them down, telling them to take it easy, or whatever words we typically use. Instead, we work at calming ourselves down, stay focused on our thought through goals for self, and all the while continuing to relate to them as they are.** Again, this is what the older brother did in the family I mentioned.

Maybe like me, you have had the good fortune from time to time of having someone relate to you in that kind of way and it has been helpful to you. When this has happened for me, I was first able to "borrow" some of their calmness, become more objectively thoughtful, and then find my own calmness and my own direction. I was then able to interrupt my reactivity and was much more helpful within the emotional system I was a part of. I became more in charge of myself and did not have the feeling that I was being run by the anxiety of others. The best kind of therapy can offer this. My wife and I will occasionally do this for each other. Happily, we tend not to get into the same outraged rant at the same time. When this happens, the calmer one can simply ask thoughtful and thought-provoking questions. The questions help us to engage our slower, cerebral cortex level thinking, and then we can do a better job of thinking things through.

Owning our anxiety and dealing with it

Paul wrote a letter to his young disciple Timothy during Paul's second and last imprisonment in Rome. He knew he was likely going to be dead soon at the hands of the Emperor Nero. He said to Timothy, who was in charge of the church in Ephesus, **"For God has not given us the spirit of fear; but of power, and love, and a sound mind." (2 Timothy 1:7)** What a potent understanding of the human situation. The Greek word for fear here is not *phobos*, but *deilos*, which is sometimes translated as "cowardice." The word for power, *dunamis*, implies the ability to function or be in charge of one's self. The word for love is *agape*, not *philos*. It is the highest form of self-sacrificing love. And sound mind refers to a thoughtful kind of self-control, free from anxiety.

This verse has been a motto of mine since adolescence when I first discovered it. It is something I have tried to live up to. Part of what makes it difficult to live up to is that we tend to deny that we are fearful and anxious. We can see it in others better than we can see it in ourselves. **Denying our anxiety will always get us into trouble. It will lead to us not being able to be in charge of our lives in the way we want (power). It will lead us to react to others and deal with them as adversaries rather than as companions whom we respect and care for (love), and it will keep us from doing an adequate job of thinking things through for ourselves and behaving in the way we want (sound mind). Paul and Bowen theory are on the same page here.**

In every tough situation—especially when we are running on automatic—we need to stop and ask ourselves, "Am I anxious here and what could that be about?" That question, coming out of our sound mind, will get us out of a lot of difficulty in life. When we become dogmatic—like the leaders in Jerusalem who questioned Peter's actions—then we are often running on automatic. **Peter feared their disapproval. He was going against orthodox dogma. He was not functioning out of his solid self. He fused emotionally with them and with those beliefs.** He didn't really think things through.

We can often use dogma to do our thinking for us. Then we are boxed in; we cannot be open to any new revelations from God. If the Jerusalem leaders had continued to insist on orthodox dogma, none of us would be here today. The church would not be here today. Probably those who followed what was then called "The Way" would have died out.

So first, we need to ask ourselves, "Am I being run by anxiety right now?" and, "What is that about?"

What our anxiety can be about may be a big list, or just a few important issues. I don't have time to list all of the options. Given that our theme today is about transitions, it is usually about some issue of loss, or some anxiety about future losses or greater demands. Stress symptoms like physical ailments, or psychological patterns, or physical acting out in addictive or unethical behaviors, can be a major clue to our anxiety.

Then, second, we need to ask, "How do I act when anxious?"

Here is a short list of anxious behaviors from Jeff Miller, who wrote *The Anxious Organization*:

- **To seek a lot of feedback, or to resist hearing it.**
- **To seek a lot of contact with others, or to withdraw.**
- **To want everyone to be happy and to please them, or to dictate what they should do or feel and impose your will.**
- **To make a snap decision, or to postpone deciding.**
- **To ignore a problem, or to exaggerate it.**
- **To micromanage your staff, or to disappear and fail to be responsibly available.**
- **To stir up conflict or to stifle it.**
- **To play politics, or to deny that politics are happening.**

Then, third, we ask ourselves, "How does my anxious behavior affect others?"

We can be clear about how other people's anxious behavior affects us, but not about how we can affect others. If you are in a leadership position, then your behavior will, almost automatically, affect others and this will account for some of their reactions to you. **Often, when a leader is unknowingly anxious, the church members catch the anxiety but focus it elsewhere, on some other issue or person within the church, or they start taking their anxiety out on each other. So when there are conflicts going on in a congregation, apparently unrelated to the leader, leaders have to ask, "What is my part in this process?" It would be a mistake to think that fights between members have nothing to do with you.**

There are always legitimate issues within the church that we will be divided over. **Anxiety does not create conflict or differences. I regard conflicts as givens in human community, especially during times of transition. But anxiety provides a fearful intensity to those conflicts.** It heightens our reactivity, so that we lose our ability to be fully in charge of ourselves, to think through issues clearly, and to be able to be open, to love, and respect those who differ from us.

When those in leadership positions deny their anxiety, this makes it less accessible to them. Their anxiety is powerful and contagious, so it spreads down through the system infecting others. The more honest we can be with ourselves, and acknowledge our anxiety, the better we can calm ourselves, and the better we can be of service to others.

In our prayers, let us always ask, "What am I anxious about today? How am I generating that sense of threat within? What is the spirit of fear leading me to do? What is that about? How will I refocus that fear and anxiety into a spirit of love?" Acts 10 and 15 tells us how the leaders at the top of the church dealt with their anxiety and this had an impact right down the whole of the church.

Thank you for your attention this morning.

Chapter 2

Going from Bad to Worse in Transitions and

How to Avoid This:

Triangles and Detriangling (Acts 11:2, 13:45, 15:2 and 5, and Galatians)

In the last talk, I spoke of how anxiety affects us and our congregations, particularly in times of transition. It is normal to become anxious at times of transition. To do a better job with it, we have to become aware of it and own it, interrupt it, and get refocused on our goals. If we don't do this, we start running on automatic.

Like Peter with the Jerusalem leaders of the early church, we can either become inconsistent around our professed principles for living in relationship with others, and/or erratic in our direction. Or, like some of the Jerusalem leaders, we can become dogmatic and inflexible. We lose touch with our ability to care for, respect, and love other people, including those who differ from us in beliefs and opinions. We stop thinking things through. We simply become reactive to whatever is going on out there because we think our number one job is to defend ourselves, and whatever we are fused with—like our version of the faith, or the way the church is organized now, or the way the church should function. I am not making a partisan political statement here. Liberals and conservatives alike can experience these threats and have these reactions. Anxiety does not belong to any one political persuasion. There can be any number of ways that we develop a sense of threat. Moreover, we fail to distinguish between what is a real threat and what is not; we may treat every change as a threat. This way of reacting will make every life transition difficult.

Anxiety will inevitably lead to triangles

When we fail to recognize these things, then we will take the next step of anxiety-based thinking. We start forming triangles. This is where transitions become even more complicated and often we don't know exactly what is going on. **We first define who our enemy is, and then we start looking for people who will be on our side, and be supportive of our cause in fighting with the enemy.** The three corners of this triangle are **Me, Those who are on my side, and Those**

who are against me. This is all it takes to have a good old church fight.

So, first of all, what is a triangle in the social sense that I am using it today? I am not asking you a geometry question. Bowen tried to use biological terms for his concepts in the theory but he couldn't come up with one for triangles even though ethologists have observed triangles in every mammalian species, not only in human beings.

Anyone want to give a stab at telling us what a triangle is? . . .

Okay. Those are good examples. Think about nearly any relationship you have, and there is probably at least one triangle lurking there. It may not be active, it may be dormant, but under the influence of anxiety, it will quickly become active.

Triangles are the basic molecule of any relationship system. Not just in families. If individual people are the atoms in a system, then triangles are the molecules. A number of triangles in a church can interlock with each other and movement in one can affect the others. Any church system you go into will have a pattern of interlocking triangles.

Any major transition that happens is going to both affect and be affected by these triangles. As transitions develop this will activate particular triangles. We can count on it. They will not all be active at any one time. Things may appear calm (like in Acts 9 that speaks of peace existing throughout the church), but given some anxiety (as occurs in Acts 10) they will be activated. For example, the day the pastor says she is moving to a new church, a number of dormant triangles immediately become active.

Sometimes we see the triangle in just a look between two people, or some other non-verbal act. Something is said by one (A) and the other two (B and C) glance at each other and kind of roll their eyes in a knowing way. That's all that happens, but the triangle is strong and active there. B & C are saying to each other something like, "Yeah, we know what he is like. He is not like us. We are different from him." B and C have a special closeness based on their agreement about A. They are the close twosome and A is the outsider. B and C may not really know all that much about each other, but they feel close to each other because of their mutual opinions about A. In triangular terms, they have a kind of pseudo-closeness. Triangles are at the heart of every betrayal, or conspiracy, and these might have started with just this kind of look, or some bit of gossip whispered between them.

This is not to say that triangles are always a wrong or bad thing. For example:

- **It is normal to want to talk with someone when you are having difficulty in another relationship. We like getting sympathy, or advice, or support from a friend when we have had a difficult encounter with someone else. Maybe we can even laugh it off with that friend and your friendship grows in response.**
- **When you and your partner are starting to get on each other's nerves, you then go to a dinner party where you see other couples interacting in a negative way. After the party, at home, you and your partner start to compare**

notes. You say, "We are not as bad as that," and you don't feel so bad about your own relationship.

- You are hoping for a promotion at work and don't get it. You call a friend and talk it over with them. The two of you try to work out what happened, what could be the boss's problems with you, or you with the boss, or whatever was going on.
- You are having difficulty relating to or managing one of your children and it helps to talk with your partner or with another parent about the issue.

In general, these triangles help us. We call them supportive relationships. They are natural and normal activities as people try to sort their way through relationship difficulties. As they progress they reveal some of the non-triangular qualities of a two-person relationship where the two people get to know more about each other as they talk, not just agree about the outside, third person. In the best case, the person we turn to can be most helpful if, in particular, they help us think about what we personally will or won't do in the situation—not just focus on the problem of the third person.

Here is a simple triangle going on with us right here, right now. I (A) am speaking to you as a group (B), about Bowen theory or Dr. Bowen (C). You and I are a twosome in terms of the theory, two corners of a triangle.

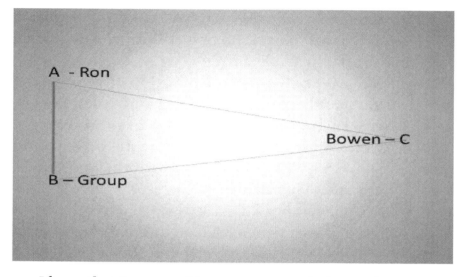

A - Ron

Bowen – C

B – Group

I hope that I am speaking to you out of what makes sense to me in my own thinking, but if I become anxious because one of you challenges me on some point, one thing I can do is to pull out an authority. I can say, "Well, Dr. Murray Bowen says . . . ." And then I am in it. I have called in an ally (C)—Murray Bowen. I have the famous systems theory originator on my side and he backs me up.

You may question me, but you are not going to question Bowen are you? He is on my side. However, you may know Bowen theory better than me and you may give a counter-quote that puts him on your side. Then the two of you will be the close twosome and I will be in the outside position. Who is on the inside or the outside can shift around in triangles.

Bowen knew this very situation would happen, especially after he was dead. A lot of us "Bowenites" (a term he hated by the way) would be running around saying, "Murray Bowen says . . . blah, blah, blah." He used to ask, **"How do**

you differentiate a self when you are dead?" It really bugged him that people could twist his meanings and act as if that is what he said. If he were here right now, he might say to me, "Ron, stop trying to put me in your corner. I am not here to defend what you have to say and I'm not sure you understand me anyway. You have to say these things to these people out of what makes sense to you, but don't try to call me in to back you up. I'll let you and them fight it out and I will enjoy watching that."

I know he would say something like this because Bowen actually said that to me one time. It was the first time I met him. A group of therapists that I was a part of back in the early 80s brought him to Vancouver to present his theory. I was, at the time, working on my first Bowen theory based book called *Family Ties That Bind*. During one of the breaks, I went up to him and said, "Dr. Bowen, I want to let you know that I am working on a popular book for laypeople on doing family of origin work based on your theory." He looked me in the eye briefly and said, "Good. Then you and they can fight and I won't have to." Then he turned and walked away. I stood there wondering what had just happened.

Bowen had developed an automatic sensitivity to triangles especially in conference settings. Right away, he got what I was trying to do. I was trying to get his permission or better yet his imprimatur for what I was writing, and he would have none of it. I was to be doing this book on my authority, not his. A typical move for him to get out of a triangle was to push the other two corners toward each other. So then, I, and his critics could fight over the issue of Bowen theory and family of origin work.

As leaders and members in the church, we do this very kind of triangle on a regular basis. **We do it with Jesus, and with Paul, and the various authors of the Bible, and even with God.**

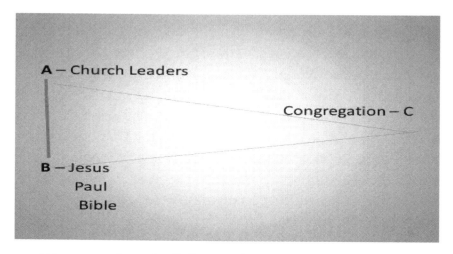

We quote them in defense of our argument. They are on our side in our disagreements with others. But then people on the other side of the argument do the same and then we are in a Bible-quoting feud, slinging verses and our interpretations at each other. I bet Jesus and Paul often wish they could step in and say what Bowen said to me.

Triangles are the basic unit of much of organizational life; they are usually at the center of our politics at all levels. I hope we all know that **being church leaders is a very political situation to be in**. I said that to one group of church leaders one time and one man said, "I wish someone would have told me that in seminary. That's the most important thing you have said today."

Let me be clear. **I am not using the term politician in a pejorative sense. Politicians are dealing with a** variety of constituencies, and each group has its own particular anxieties that it is looking for support for from the leader of the party. They say to the leader, "I/We want you to represent our point of view, our position on this issue."

Bowen theory is not about politics as such, nor is it a substitute for political action, but it can make us better politicians. It helps us to understand what is going on emotionally around political issues and the ramifications of our own actions within that arena.

Triangling is a normal human activity, and it is sometimes very helpful, but more often triangles can make difficult situations much worse and their presence, and their proliferation, are an indication of significant anxiety within an emotional system like a church. They can make times of transition go from bad to worse.

As I said earlier, triangles typically have two inside positions and one outside position. One or more people can be in each corner. So it could be three groups of people, or two groups around a divisive issue (the third corner). In one version of a triangle, these positions can be chronic and unchanging, or in another, the people in them can switch around depending on the issue or the circumstance.

If the two inside people are in conflict, the outside person is often happy to stay outside. If the two insiders are great, close friends, the outside person may want to get in and either be a part of their warm twosome, or maybe replace one or the other, as in a love triangle. Shifting positions around can happen in subtle ways and we can feel it happen if we are in a triangle where, for example, we had been the favored, inside person and then someone else gets the attention we want. We feel the threat of loss of closeness or loss of love—usually, we call this jealousy.

Here is a longer example. If the Chair of the church education committee (A) comes into conflict with the chair of the budget committee (B), it is normal that they each look for you (C) as the leader to take their side. If you do take a side, then one side sees you as a friendly and strong leader, and the other side sees you as the enemy, as weak-kneed or feeble-minded, and unable to take a stand. Does that sound familiar to anybody here? As a politician you are always going to have someone unhappy with you, unless you are really good at smooth talking and, might I say even lying, or finding someone else to blame for the outcome of things.

Both sides have a certain amount of anxiety around the loss of your support as a leader and they want to see their own agenda upheld by you. They are looking for the leader to stand by them, to represent their point of view. There is a sense of threat involved. Especially in cases like this, anxiety breeds triangles.

To continue the example, here is just one way it might happen—but realize this very situation could go so many directions in terms of triangles. The options are nearly endless and often surprising. Let's say Sue (A), the chair of the education committee, goes to Bill (B) the clergy leader of the church. She lays out to him what she believes is a fantastic vision for the church school along with some specific program ideas, but she knows that Joe (C), the chair of the budget committee does not believe in programs like this or the increased budgets that go with them. He simply wants teachers to teach the Bible, period. He thinks nothing "fancy" is needed to do this. He says, "Just read the Bible and teach it." Bill asks Sue if she has tried to discuss this with Joe, and she says no, that she finds Joe difficult to talk to. Then she tells Bill that she has spoken with Marie, the Assistant Pastor in the church (another, interlocking A-B-C triangle), and that Marie supports Sue's idea enthusiastically. Marie thought that Bill would support it too.

Sue is looking for people to help her with her anxiety in relation to Joe. She takes the anxiety she has in relation to Joe and puts it into the relationship, first with Marie, and then with Bill. She does this in the hope of getting Bill's help with her anxiety, and maybe both Bill and Marie will argue with Joe on her behalf. **If she didn't have the anxiety around dealing with Joe, she wouldn't need to go to these others.** She would deal directly with him. No triangle needed.

This is a common maneuver in church politics as well as in family life, friendships, social life, work life, or wherever. Sue is doing an end-run on Joe, or going over his head, or trying to leave him out of the loop. Teenagers do this with their parents when they are looking for permission to do something not previously allowed. They may try to play one parent off against the other. These are standard lines or feelings when triangles have been activated in a system. If Joe knew about this, he would likely be upset. He might say, "She is playing politics here." Triangles often involve secrets and they reveal a breakdown in a two-person relationship.

Bowen said that two-person relationships, like between Sue and Joe, are very unstable. It is difficult for two people to go very far before one of them gets anxious about some difference between them and attempts to bring in a third person. Note your daily discussions with the people you are close to. Do you talk only about yourselves, or your relationship with each other, or do you find yourself talking about others? Sue, for whatever reasons, gets uneasy about trying to work things out with the "more opinionated" Joe. It is an unstable relationship for this reason.

Let's take the example further and bring in more inter-locking triangles. Say a wife and husband (Sue, A—the same one who is Chair of the education committee at the church, and her husband Arnie, B) are arguing about one of their usual unresolved topics. Then she says in frustration, "Oh, you are just like the guy from Mars that I read about in this book. You are so typical. You better pay attention to what you are doing and change. Here, read this book about how men are from Mars." She appeals to an outside authority for help (another C). Arnie feels supplanted by a book author of all people. Sue seems closer to the author than she is to him. At this point, since this has happened often before, he blows up saying, "You and your books. I'm done with all of this." He storms out of the house, calls his buddy Jim, and says, "Can you meet me at the bar? I am so upset with Sue I don't know what to do anymore. I am thinking of leaving her."

So then, Jim and Arnie get together and have a few beers (another A-B-C). Jim tries to be a helpful, neutral person, as he knows he should, but he has never really liked Sue and he can't help but sympathize with Arnie. Essentially, he is on Arnie's side and besides, he has trouble with his own wife around the same kinds of issues. The more beer they drink the more they commiserate with one another about women in general.

After Arnie leaves the house, Sue calls her mother Arlene in tears (another A-B-C). She tells mother about their fight and about how it seems to her now like they fight all the time. And Arnie is so mean to her. This is the first time mother has heard the details although she had a sense they were having difficulties. She says to Sue, "Well dear, this is just what I predicted to you when you said you wanted to marry Arnie. I told you he was not the man for you, and only now are you seeing that I was right. Your father agreed with me too. I don't want to say, 'I told you so,' but I am afraid you have made your bed and you are going to have to lie in it. You are just going to have to find a way to get along with Arnie and make him happy. That is your job as a wife." In essence, Arlene takes Arnie's side in the conflict. Sue feels more alone and upset.

After this encounter, Sue calls her best friend Miranda (another A-B-C) and tells her all that has just happened. Miranda is divorced, and down on men in general and tells Sue to give up trying to make this marriage work. She says that Sue's mother just wants her to be a doormat for her husband and that women don't need to be this way anymore. She tells Sue to forget what her mother says and to leave Jim and her life will get better.

The other people, Jim, and Arlene, and Miranda each have their own anxiety around these two person issues, in their own lives, and they counsel Arnie and Sue with their own fix-it solutions to these anxious circumstances.

So when Sue goes to Bill for support in dealing with Joe, the budget committee chair, she already has all of these triangles sitting there in her immediate emotional background; she is already feeling vulnerable and like she is a victim in relation to tough, difficult men, and in relation to an authority like her mom. She wants someone to take on her anxiety and fight for her. But while talking with him, she realizes that Bill is not going to stand up for her with Joe, she becomes first tearful, and then angry. Bill tries to calm her down and says something like, "Rome wasn't built in a day," and that she has to move more slowly with these kinds of ambitious educational plans. And then Sue, feeling her frustration boiling over, begins to lambast Bill and says she is done with "this stupid church," "it is male-dominated and holds women back," and that she is resigning from the education committee and leaving the church and as far as she is concerned they can all just "stuff it." And Sue storms out of the office.

What Sue doesn't know is that her mother Arlene (who is also a member in the church) has already called Bill (another A-B-C) about her argument with Sue and she tells Bill what she said and she would like for Bill to reiterate this message if Sue comes to him. She tells him that, "Sue needs to be toughened up."

Arlene and her husband are big donors to the church and they are central figures in the church system (another A-B-C). Arlene has also called Bill's wife Mabel (another A-B-C) and told her the story and what she expects of Bill. Arlene carries a lot of political weight in the congregation and with Bill. Mabel is anxious for Bill's career and doesn't want him to do anything to jeopardize it. Arlene expects Bill to support her in this critical stance with her daughter Sue and she is lining up her ducks. Bill is quite hesitant to contradict Arlene or counsel Sue in any way that would oppose Arlene, but he does resent Arlene's intrusion into all of these matters. In fact, he just wants to be in the outside position in all of this political stuff. This is what he hates about being a pastor. He would rather that these people slug it out with each other and not try to involve him. He also is highly anxious. He feels the danger that it could all come down on his head somehow. He suspects—because it has happened before—that Arlene has called Mabel and now he is even dreading going home because of what he is going to encounter there with Mabel. He doesn't want to have a fight with her too.

But Bill does know that he can take some of his frustration out on his assistant, Marie (another A-B-C). And so he lays in to her for taking Sue's side in the argument with Joe. He tells her she can't be doing this kind of thing: she can't go behind his back and undercut his authority, and that she should go learn something about systems theory and that she should read this book he has on systems in congregations. Also, he begins thinking about how he can work in the phrase, "Blessed are the peacemakers" into this Sunday's sermon.

At about the same time Bill has a chance encounter with his new bishop, Markus. Markus had been a seminary Dean and Bill decides to take some of his frustration out on the bishop. Bill says to him, "Why didn't you people in seminary prepare us for what we would encounter in the parish? What kind of a world do you live in? Don't you know what it is like out here on the front lines?" And on it goes. The triangles can be endless. See the diagram of all of these triangles on the next page.

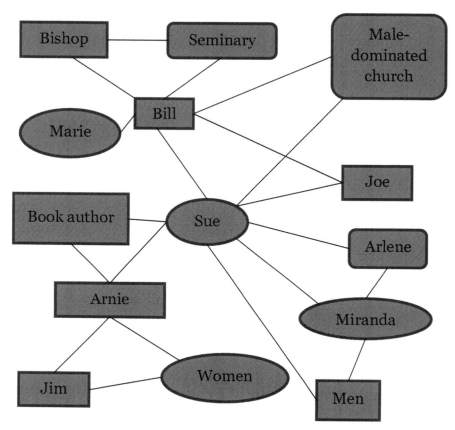

Each of these triangles represents possible or imminent transition points where there will be upset people in the system. A possible divorce, a possible church fight between Joe's group and Sue's group, and possible leaving of an important church member, a possible reduction in giving, or something worse, in a difference of opinion with a key church member. And things could snowball even further in the potential fallout from these things. The bishop could wonder about Bill's stability. **Two-person relationships**

are unstable and they almost automatically convert into triangles when people get anxious.

People are looking for help with their anxiety. That is why triangles exist. If there were no anxiety, the problematic triangles would not happen. But how likely is that? **One of the goals of Bowen theory is that people can achieve a one-to-one relationship with each other.** They can deal openly and directly with each other, keeping their anxiety about the encounter at bay, and not need to triangle. I will say more about this later.

I have greatly simplified these things in these examples. **A congregation is a vast emotional field of interlocking triangles (much more complicated than I have described here), and, just like in the mobile, as someone has difficulty in one particular relationship, it is going to have a ripple effect through the system.**

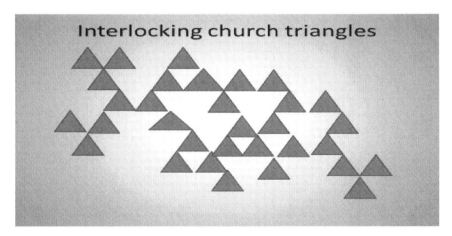

Interlocking church triangles

Sometimes there is a tsunami wave effect in the relationship system of the church, and the whole church is affected. Imagine some huge, quivering amoebic cell and when it gets touched over on one side, it shakes through the whole cell in recoil. Whatever transitions are going on will get more complicated and difficult when triangles are involved.

So, I suppose this kind of thing is not really familiar to anyone here today. Your life is not like this is it? Right? Oh? Okay. It is familiar. Triangles are never ending. And in times of transition, when people are already anxious, they can get really stirred up and become chaotic.

I know you are thinking right now, "All right Ron. You have described my life. Now what should I do about it? You aren't going to leave us dangling with this whole description are you?" Well, yes, I am. For the time being.

Back to the story in Acts 10. Peter had this great revelation in his vision (that he should not call anyone common or unclean) and the door is opened to the gentiles becoming saved through Jesus Christ. He realizes that the requirements of the law do not first have to be fulfilled for gentiles to become Christians; they do not have to enter the Christian faith through the Jewish door of the Torah. They do not have to observe the Jewish laws and traditions that were once commanded by God. Astounding!

However, as revealed in the Gospels, we all know that Peter was slow to think things through and he had his usual problem with consistency, with being able to stand firm on a position that he took. Luke does not tell us the whole story around this issue and I am going to say a lot about what developed in the next talk. Right now, we just need to remember that Peter backed off of his position when the church leaders in Jerusalem, who were still committed to the Jewish law (things like the cleanliness rituals, forbidden foods, table fellowship with gentiles, and most important, circumcision) as a requirement for becoming a Christian, became involved.

In other words, what had been a clear statement of the gospel of God's grace for all became muddied through the triangles that developed in the early church. Peter lost focus for how he wanted to be. People were anxious in this transition. The beliefs they had always lived by were threatened. This is completely understandable. This is a big deal. Of course, people were anxious. In addition, there must have been many rumors going on, a lot of people talking to each other about other people, and little direct conversation. I am sure there were people saying that Peter had gone over the edge and needed to be put back on the right path. They may have said to each other, "Poor Peter. He is not the most thoughtful guy and he has trouble being consistent. We have to pull him back into the fold of true faith. Who knows what his position would lead to if the consequences were ignored?"

The self in the triangle

There are several things that we can focus on as a resource in a triangle and when we feel anxious. The triangle is raising a question that only you can answer. It is not about managing others, or about the various personalities involved and wishing they would change somehow, or sending them off to therapy, or getting them to read a book. **We all know that we can't change others, but we forget this when we get anxious. We try to change them so we can feel less anxious.**

The question raised is one of personal principle and of solid beliefs. Where do we ourselves stand in situations like this? What principles guide our own functioning in relation to all of these people and the anxious concerns they have? It is not an issue of managing them, which will likely involve more triangles and more emotional upset, but an issue of how we will be with them in the midst of this anxious turmoil. Will we add to the turmoil of all of these interlocking triangles out of our own anxiety, or will we bring something different? And what principles of relationship functioning do we need to have to do this?

This is where Bowen theory becomes especially helpful. First, we have to be able to see the triangles. In training therapists for clinical work, and clergy in my leadership seminars, this was one of the first things they needed to learn. **It is so automatic for us to step into triangles, under the guise of what we call "being helpful." We don't even see that a triangle was going on and that we were participating out of our own anxious desire to help.**

I talk about this process a great deal in my book *Couples in Conflict*.

Couples in Conflict
A Family Systems Approach
to Marriage Counseling

RONALD W. RICHARDSON

When people go to see a therapist, or talk to their pastor or other church leader about some interpersonal problem they face, they may spend most of their time talking about "the other person." They describe him or her, or them, to the helper. And if the helper buys in to this presentation of the problem, then the triangular process takes over.

Once the trainees began to understand what an emotional triangle was, and how they participated in it by focusing on "the other person(s)," and what brought that about, they were on the road to becoming better therapists and pastors. They also began to see all of the triangles they were a part of in their daily lives and would exclaim, "They're everywhere! We are surrounded by them!" This was true, and it called for a major change in the way they lived their daily lives.

Triangles typically involve three roles or positions sometimes called, in popular terms, **Persecutor, Victim, and Rescuer**. When we are active in a triangle, it is usually in one of these three positions and, of course, we can move around, taking different positions at different times. Sue would have seen herself as the Victim, Joe as the Persecutor, and Bill as the Rescuer. But it did not stay this way. **Rescuers can easily become victims or persecutors. Victims can become persecutors, and persecutors can become victims.** Each position is other-focused; it is about what we are doing to or for others or what they are doing to or for us, and how we are trying to help or change one of the other two, or help them sort out their relationship. Therapists and church caregivers easily step in to the role of being rescuers, but that can change.

As rescuers, we see someone oppressing another person or manipulating them, and we try to sort out things between them. We give advice to one about how to relate to the other one. We make ourselves responsible for what is going on between the two (or more) other people. Or, as persecutors, we want to punish someone for their actions, or hurt them, or make them submit to our wishes, and we resist anyone like a rescuer trying to change us. As victims, we can feel helpless and hopeless, unable to change anything in our lives—we think our lives are what other people make them, or make us to be. We depend on rescuers coming to our aid.

In triangles, we typically focus on other peoples' personalities, or often on what we think are their intentions or motivations. We diagnose them and

what we think their problems are. We can go on forever diagnosing other people's personality problems, or their evil intentions, and thinking about what they need to do to change. However, they are likely doing the same thing with you, and they may be actively trying to change your personality (and its attendant intentions, motivations, and behavior) or just wishing you would change—maybe they do it by praying for you.

If you are in any kind of a problematic mess, think triangles. If you are confused about what is going on, think triangles. Often when I got confused when doing therapy, I would try to find what triangles existed that I didn't know about. Figure out what triangles you are in, be thorough, and see what your position is in them, and then how you will have to change your own behavior. If you do this, you have made a good start on creating change for yourself.

Defining self within triangles—being a resource and detriangling

I am going to say a lot more about this in the next talk, but for now, in dealing with the major triangles, we have to define ourselves to the others who are involved. We take **what is called an I-position. Doing this means we can**:

- **Calm our emotionally reactive selves and engage our thinking.**
- **Then figure out the triangles we are in and who is playing what part.**
- **Attempt to understand what might be the sources of anxiety in the issue for yourself**

and others—although you are not going to define this to or for them; this is just for self.

- Own up for ourselves the other-focused position we have taken in the triangle.
- Stop diagnosing others and focusing on their problems (their personalities or intentions or motivations)—even if, and especially, they are doing that to us.
- Identify (only for ourselves) what issues are involved (rather than personalities).
- Think through, as clearly as possible, our own position on the issue (which may take some time).
- Stay connected with (actively talking with and listening to) all of the people involved in the triangle.
- And finally, make our own thinking about the issue (not the people and their personalities or motivations) known to others.

The basic principle involved here is that you as the helper cannot change the relationship between any two (or more) other people. Bill could not change the relationship between Sue and Joe or any of the other relationships in the example. You have a relationship only with the person who has come to you for help. You are not going to change even that person, **but you can be a resource to that person**. You can help them think through what they are up against and what they might do about it.

So if I were Bill, in the extended example above, or even all the people Sue turned to like Marie, or her mother Arlene, or Miranda. Or if I was any other helping person, even a friend, **all I can do is offer Sue my ability to stay out of the triangle and help Sue think through her own part in the problem**.

Bill could say, "Sue, let's talk about this difficulty you are having discussing things with Joe. What do you find difficult about that?" She says, "He is so stern and dogmatic." Notice how she has focused it back over to Joe, identifying what his problem is. Bill can say, "Okay. When you are up against someone that you think is that way, what happens to you?" She says, "They won't talk in a reasonable way with me." She has again deflected from herself over to Joe's problem. Bill says, "You may not notice Sue that I asked about you, not about Joe." She says, "Me? Well no one can talk to a person like that." Again, she is not looking at herself. She claims anyone would have this problem. She is keeping it in the triangle still. Bill can say, "Well I can grant you that some people may have trouble talking with Joe, but really, I am asking about what is difficult for you. What happens for you?" She says, "Well, I have never thought about that. Hmmm. You know, he is just like my dad. I could never get through to him either." Bill says, "Okay, that is interesting and that is probably where you started having this difficulty. It might even carry over to people like your husband?" She says, "Yes, it does. He can be hard-headed too." Now she back into triangular thinking.

Bill says, "Well Sue I would like to talk with you about you when you have this experience. We can talk about you and your dad later. By the way, I think that would be a very profitable thing to do. But, right now let's stick with you and Joe. Again, I am asking you, what happens to you when you try to talk about your plans with Joe?" Then Sue says,

"Okay. I think I get what you are asking. What happens to me when I am trying to talk to a person like Joe? Good question. You know, I have never thought about that. Let me see . . . ."

There would be many questions that Bill could ask to help her think about the kind of place she gets herself into when dealing with a guy like Joe. The point is that **Bill is being a resource to her by lending his thinking brain to her, helping her to think about her own inner processes, and how she ends up feeling powerless with particular people in her life**. She may never get Joe to agree with her about funding her program but at least she will, at some point, be able to stay in the same room with him and explore, one-on-one, all of what is involved. And Joe will have a new experience with her.

Like Bill, we get ourselves de-triangled by doing this kind of thing. As we do this, people might focus on us as the problem. They say, "You don't get it. It is this other person that is the problem, not me." Then we can ask them to define themselves on the issue. We do this by asking as many genuine questions as we can, trying to think through their position with them, and trying to evoke their own thinking behind their position. **If we can do this in a neutral way—by which I mean we are not trying to change them, or convince them they are wrong, but just interested in their own experience and thinking and behavior—they will profit from the kind of thoughtfulness they are invited into, and quite often, appreciate it.**

When you are the third person, as in this example, this is the way we can be of help to those who come to us. **Good** friends do this for each other rather than just playing "Ain't It Awful" with the person who complains to you. **The point is to be able to be a resource to the friend so that they can go to the person they are having difficulty with and be different.**

We want to be able to get to one-on-one relationships with the people involved. **So Sue is able to be with Joe and do her part in attempting to talk things through rather than avoid him, or try to enlist others to do it for her. Then Sue will feel the best about herself, and it is a considerate way to deal with Joe. She can be a more solid self with him by taking her own I-position with him.**

Let me be clear. Taking an I-position in a triangle is not going to settle everything, but it is going to set you in a better direction. Things might even get worse for a while, but if you can still define self and stay related to those who differ from you, and then you are on the road to a resolution—eventually. This is what happened with the older brother in the family I mentioned earlier. Once he declared his position, there was a strong reaction against him. Other family members got angry and called him names. He stood his ground, listened to them, did not argue with them, or attack them, or react to their reactions. When they eventually stopped reacting as a result, and started thinking, they either saw the wisdom of his decision or knew they could not change him, and were able to work out a new agreement between them.

As you respectfully listen to the others, and think through their positions with them, **it might be that your own thinking begins to change. We have to be open**

to that possibility, and that is fine. For example, Sue might have to reflect on what she was bringing to the encounter with Joe that got him reactive to her. We can then refine, or redefine, our own position. She might see that she had come on with Joe in a way that he considered "pushy," and that he had reacted stubbornly to that. That would be Joe's issue but she might need to take it into account. She can look at what difficulties or concerns are raised by Joe's position, and then maybe thinking out loud with him—usually through asking questions. The point is we are trying to figure out what makes sense to us on the issue while also staying related to others who differ from us as we do this.

Maintaining the one-to-one relationship in times of transition

We Christians have a verse we often like to quote in church. Jesus said, "Wherever two or three are gathered together in my name, there am I in the midst of them." We sometimes cynically say, wherever two or three are gathered together in his name, especially in times of change, there is going to be conflict, trouble, and triangles. In this way of thinking, **we are likely to label the church as dysfunctional—which is not actually a term I use, ever, whether it be a family or a congregation. It is a useless diagnostic term**. What we label as dysfunctional is actually a kind of functionality in which people are attempting to deal with their anxious concerns. It just doesn't actually get us anywhere beyond trying to spread out the anxiety. This is the point though; people are trying, as best they can, to deal with their anxiety, often by involving others in triangles.

The problem in a community with differences is not the conflict itself, it is the anxiety we attach to the conflict. Then, when this happens, we see each other as adversaries; we personalize and ascribe evil motivations to the other. And they tend to do this to us.

Trying to tamp down differences and conflict is one of the ways we attempt to reduce our level of anxiety. We call it the peace at any price approach. We will often choose that over the kind of polarized conflict that can happen. However, then the conflict goes underground and it is harder to deal with. **We forget that difference and conflict is normal in human relationships. This is part of how we grow and change. Without these elements, we would likely be dead as an organization.** There would be no church, or any other kind of organization, without conflict. Whatever else is meant in the Bible by the concepts of unity and peace (like in the Gospel of John), I am sure it does not mean the obliteration of differences between members of the faith, as if each person had no separate ideas of his or her own. The issue is how to do it and not have painful and angry divisions.

When church members are fully and intelligently engaged with one another, and when they care about outcomes, and have strong convictions, it is natural for them to have some clash of beliefs. It is only when we handle our conflicts badly that we have negative outcomes. Then major resentment builds, blame increases, people feel hurt and damaged, distance between people grows, and community falls apart. In addition, in these circumstances, as anxiety intensifies and triangles proliferate, there are always people who will be blameworthy; people we can point to and say they are the problem. Then the emotional energy of the church will focus on these people.

When we blame, as several people did in the Sue-Joe-Bill example, we deny any responsibility for our own part in the emotional process. If we claim the position of being the good guys, of being on the correct side of an issue, then we are powerless to change anything. We exaggerate the power of the other person, or we give them greater power, but they are thinking the same thing about us. We get nowhere. In blaming and scapegoating, we engage in a contemporary form of human sacrifice just like the old biblical scapegoat.

If we can have our differences, and relate to one another without being anxious and reactive, and forming triangles, these negative things will not happen to our community. We can know serious matters are at stake, but we also take each other seriously and believe in the good intentions of the others. If I believed that I cannot be related to anyone who differs from me on serious matters, I would not be married, and I would not have a friend, or live in community, or be a citizen in my own country. I expect to go to my grave with differences between my wife and me, after 45 years of marriage, still unresolved, but we still love each other and debate our differences. Many happy couples cancel out each other's vote in political elections. And they laugh about it.

What I don't have time to go into in these talks is that much of our emotional intensity in serious contemporary conflicts are our efforts to right wrongs that go way back in our personal history—it has to do with our family of origin. This is where our emotional intensity often comes from. Sue's issues with Joe began with her relationship with her father and mother. I have shown how this happens in many of my books, especially in *Becoming a Healthier Pastor*. We personalize conflict because for so long, it has felt so intensely personal to us. We are really, deep down and usually unconsciously, fighting old battles.

The early church, as we hear about it in Acts, in its first ecumenical conference in Jerusalem, in the midst of major, truly revolutionary change, opened up its triangles, improved the one-to-one relationships, and was able to negotiate its way through the difficulties. We can do it too. More on this in the next talk.

Chapter 3

Making even Difficult Transitions Work Better:

Differentiation of Self

(Acts 15:8–10, Galatians 2:11–14)

Paul in Antioch and Jerusalem

As you may know, Luke does not give us the whole story in Acts about the great, revolutionary transition that took place around the proclamation of the gospel to gentiles and how they could come to Christ. You remember that Paul fills in some of the picture for us.

Galatians 2 is one of the great Pauline passages. It is the Magna Carta of Christian freedom proclaimed during a time of great uncertainty and confusion in the early church. As he says in the letter, **"For freedom Christ has set us free."** Paul takes on those who would, as he says, pervert the gospel by making it subject to the law of the Torah. This letter is full of autobiographical detail as well as laying down the principles that made Christianity into a world religion and not just another Jewish sect.

We have to remember Paul's uncertain status as an apostle in the early church due to his own history. He did not know Jesus during his earthly ministry. He was not part of the original twelve disciples. He had been a leading Pharisee, the group angriest with Jesus and the group Jesus condemned the most. He was a man who knew the Law backward and forward and followed it to the letter. And not only that, he had been a persecutor of the early Christians, present at the stoning of Stephen. So in the eyes of many he was greatly suspect.

In Galatians 2, Paul recounts the proceedings of the first great ecumenical conference of Christians in Jerusalem (this is also described in Acts 15). Paul has decided to go to Jerusalem, taking with him his companions Barnabas, a Jewish Christian, and Titus, a Greek Christian and a gentile. Paul went there to seek confirmation that he is a legitimate apostle and that the gospel he preaches is legitimate, and to verify, as he says, "that he was not running in vain." He doesn't want to be perceived as just some renegade tent evangelist out there doing whatever pleases him and making up a gospel of his own.

In addition, just as important, he wants to address, and hoped to resolve what has become potentially a major split in the church. The central theological question before them is, "Do the gentiles have to become Jews before they can become Christians?" In particular, "Do they have to be circumcised as a sign of following the Law?" You remember that his convert Timothy, who was a Greek but born of a Jewish mother, requested to be circumcised and Paul went along with that. But the gentile Titus wasn't interested in circumcision and Paul said no problem: "For freedom Christ has set us free." We are no longer required to follow Jewish rules.

However, Paul says, "some people spied out our freedom" and tried to enslave us again to the Law, demanding that Titus be circumcised. But when he brought this issue before the pillars of the church at this conference in Jerusalem, he opened up this triangle. The pillars agreed with Paul, gave him the right hand of fellowship, confirmed his apostolic ministry to the Greeks, and that, in particular, the way to Christ did not go through the Torah. What a momentous decision!

Then, Paul gives us a flashback, telling of the time that Peter came to Antioch—which, you remember, is where the followers of Jesus were first called Christians. Peter had joined in with Paul in eating with the gentile Christians until James, the bishop of Jerusalem, criticized him. James could be considered the hardliner of the early church, insisting as much as possible on following the Law. In this encounter, Peter pulled back, and refrained from eating with the gentiles. Peter's problem with steadfastness reappeared. He feared the circumcision party and so the other Jewish Christians joined in with Peter, including even Barnabas. When Paul saw this, he felt not only personally betrayed but also angry on behalf of the gospel.

Paul knew he had to do something, so without hostility, he openly confronted Peter in his hypocrisy. He moved into a person-to-person relationship with Peter. He said to Peter in front of them all, face to face, that it can't work this way. Does he believe the gospel, and indeed his own vision from God that told him to eat with the gentile Cornelius, or not? And Peter then agrees with Paul, and says he is right. He rejoined the table fellowship with the gentile believers.

Now, after this historical digression, Paul returns to the first ecumenical council in Jerusalem, which included James—the bishop. Peter gives the winning speech to the assembly confirming Paul's message. It is agreed that, "God has made no distinction between us" and that the yoke of the law is once and for all thrown off of believers. We are all saved by faith and not by following the Law. James agrees with and confirms this message, although, in his own way. He has to do it by giving a long sermon on the prophet Amos.

Paul puts an end to the power of this triangle. He does so by surfacing an argument that some might have found uncomfortable or embarrassing to air in public. Failing to do this would allow a major triangle to continue to confuse the issues in the church. The new guy in the faith takes on the old guy Peter who has always had a problem with consistency, and who can be swayed emotionally by others, or by the voice of an authority like James. Paul says we no longer make our decisions based on the law, but simply on the basis of believing in Jesus. As he says in Galatians 3:28, "there is neither Jew nor Greek, neither male nor female," etc. **The church is successfully passing through a major transition.**

Part of what this story tells me is that robust arguments with one another about the meaning of our faith are fine. They are important because we all care about the truth. Only we need to do it face to face, not by innuendo or rumor and triangling. I can just imagine that, back then, there were various groups who would huddle together and talk about the others who disagreed with them, behind their back. They would focus on personalities. They may have speculated about the motives of the others and diagnosed what their problem was. This is the kind of triangular politicking that often goes on in our churches today, and in our workplaces, and our social circles. **Later in the Galatians letter comes Paul's famous instruction reiterating the Great Commandment to "love one another" and warning them against this kind of triangular behavior, saying that "if you bite and devour one another, take heed lest you be consumed by one another."**

I quote this passage at the beginning of my book *Polarization and the Healthier Church*, because this is just what is happening in our society as well as in our church today.

POLARIZATION
AND THE
HEALTHIER CHURCH

APPLYING BOWEN FAMILY
SYSTEMS THEORY TO CONFLICT
AND CHANGE IN SOCIETY
AND CONGREGATIONAL LIFE

RONALD W. RICHARDSON

In this book, among other extended examples, I tell about how the United Church in the Vancouver Presbytery approached its debates about the ordination of gay people. Quite unexpectedly to them as well as for me, I had the leaders of the two sides, pro and con, show up together in my nine-month training sessions in Bowen theory and ministry, a year before the vote was to be taken in the Presbytery. Neither of them knew the other had signed up for the course. In that chapter I tell about how the debate developed in that Presbytery as a result of that training experience and that for me as an observer, how impressed I was with the way those two leaders managed themselves in the debate and vote that followed after their experience in my program.

In Paul's Galatian story, we see a verification of Bowen theory around managing self in emotional circumstances. In particular, **Paul is demonstrating differentiation of self. He is defining himself in relation to other important people in the faith, directly, at the face-to-face level**. As a result, Peter is then able to define himself openly, finally, and when the great conference happens in Jerusalem this self-definition ended up winning the day for the gospel. But it was not easy; there was lots of opposition, and it must have been tough for them both.

Differentiation of self

Dr. Bowen did not invent his eight theoretical concepts de novo, out of thin air. He based them on direct observations of the way people actually behave in close emotional relationships. His concepts are about functional human realities. These realities have been a part of human history from the beginning. They describe how we normally function in relationships, how we get ourselves in trouble, and how we can get ourselves out of trouble, eventually.

Differentiation is the ability to function more as a separate, autonomous self and be guided less by other people in the emotional system. We differentiate a self out of the emotional fusion of the system, not out of the system itself.

It does not mean emotionally distancing from others. It is easy to be a self when we get away from others—that is part of why we distance, to get self back, and lower our anxiety. Differentiation is about a different way of being with others.

Differentiation of self is the key concept in relation to creating change. It is the primary resource for church leaders, whether they are official, office-holding leaders or not. Anyone who works at differentiating a self within a congregation will automatically become a leader in the church. But it is not easy.

First, it takes a lower level of anxiety. Letting his anxiety rule him, I can imagine Paul wanting to stay away from Jerusalem, keep his distance, and not speak directly with the leaders there. He must have feared a possible negative outcome around both of his goals. However, he did not avoid them. **Secondly**, he calmly and respectfully went before them saying, "This is what I believe and what I have been doing." He openly defined himself. He clearly stated his beliefs and the basis of those beliefs. He gets the two festering issues (of his apostolic authority and his gospel of grace) out into the open. **Third**, he stayed emotionally connected to the others. He did not just make a declaration and then disappear. That self-definition evoked others to say what they believed. A decision had to be made one way or another around Paul's authority, his message, and what he was doing in the gentile world. The argument was not about personalities and motivations. It was about consistency on the critical theological issues involved.

Note that the titular head of the church, James, did not bring this on. James was just going with the flow that reflected his ethnocentric reality in Jerusalem. In addition, as we learn later in Acts, the church was having great difficulty with the unconverted Jews in the city. It was Paul the outsider, the one whose standing was more questionable, who laid it before them. James had to develop personally and change his own thinking and understanding as a result.

Because we are each a part of the church emotional system, **any self-defining effort we make, presenting it to others, will provoke further thinking and discussion by others. If this is done in the spirit of respecting and loving one another, rather than "biting and devouring one another,"** the outcome will ultimately be a better one even though there may be temporary turmoil. Issues will be clarified. Just being calm and clear in your own thinking comes first, and then letting that be known in direct relationships.

We all have different ways of getting ourselves calm. There are many different techniques. The popular press is full of these techniques. We have to find what works for us. My personal goal, if I remember to do it, is to get myself calm by relaxing my face muscles (the face reflects our inner thinking), and with three deep breaths, calming and slowing my breathing. It is so easy to lose that calmness in the heat of the moment—at least this is true for me—that we have to be practiced at it. "Being mindful" is one contemporary term for what I am talking about.

How we are thinking about things is also critical. When I am acting out of my anxiety during these times of difficult transitions, and heading in an unhelpful direction, I start thinking about who is right and who is wrong. I start blaming others. I think about who is on my side, and who is my enemy. I think about my opponents' problems, or how screwed up they are, and how they need to change, what their real motivations and intentions are, and so forth. All of those feeling-based, other focused opinions get me more upset and more ready to fight with them. They are not really my solid, self-focused thoughts about an issue and my understanding of it. Every argument by others gets me going with my counter-argument and I have my speech ready before they have finished theirs. I am reacting to them rather than defining myself.

When we have calmed ourselves, then that can be catching. Others will have a better chance of calming themselves. **Calmness can be contagious just like anxiety is contagious. We lower the intensity in our voice and the energy in our gestures.** This is different from telling others to be calm. That often does not work. Often, others get reactive when being told to "calm down." They say angrily, "Don't you tell me to calm down." Instead, we are just calmer ourselves, as we relate to them, and leave them to figure out how to do this for themselves. How they are is not our job. We just have to be in charge of ourselves when we are with them.

After we calm ourselves, we have to think about and clarify for ourselves, "What do I really believe? What important principles are at stake here?" This may take some time and careful deliberation rather than just reacting at a gut level. Being thoughtful is critical in defining self.

Also, as a part of this, **we need to think about the beliefs of others and be clear as to what they are. We do this not to argue their beliefs with them but simply to connect with them and demonstrate that we understand their concerns. It helps to attempt to state to the others our understanding of their beliefs, and ask them if this understanding is correct.**

Is it accurate? I ask does my statement cover all of the bases as to what is important in their understanding.

In these sorts of situations, we often hear people say to the other, "I just don't understand you." What they mean is, "I don't agree with you." They fear that "understanding" means "agreement." In this effort, as we try to understand them, where do we get ourselves anxious in response and start to up the emotional ante and argue with them? Where does this anxiety actually come from for you, not for them? Listen for triangles and attempt to get them out in the open by asking questions (not by accusing them of triangling!). Also, who is pursuing whom and who is distancing?

The point of doing this is not to change them or argue with them. Sometimes, what is called communication with others is often just another way of arguing with them, trying to get them to agree with us. This kind of communication often fails and becomes frustrating for both parties. Around divisive and polarized issues, this kind of communication ends up angering everyone.

At its best, this effort could be understood as **evoking the best thinking of others by asking questions of clarification**—saying something like, "Help me to understand what you are saying here? Do you mean . . . ." "Do you mean . . . " type questions are very useful. Or, "Am I understanding you correctly that you are saying . . . ?" Taking this kind of interested stance is also a part of differentiation. We are deciding where to put our interest rather than reacting to the others. When we are reacting to others, then others are deciding where we will focus our thinking. Our reactivity puts them in charge of us. Thinking about good "Do you mean . . ." questions also helps us to calm down.

Self-focus within the emotional system and differentiation of self

Here is an essential point. **We have to ask ourselves, what am I doing in the emotional system that could provoke the anxiety of others and stimulate their reactivity?** This would be a helpful thought for Sue to get to at some point. If she knew more about how she approached others to get the reaction she got from them, perhaps she would be able to get a different reaction and get further in accomplishing her goals. **We can be very clear about what others are doing to us, or how we think they are behaving with us, and how we think they are angering or upsetting us, but we are usually not so clear about what our impact is on them.** This is different from self-blame. This does not mean that we are responsible for how they act, just as they are not responsible for our reactions. Either one of us can step out of this cycle of reactivity if we can calm ourselves and get clearer in our own thinking, but we do have a responsibility to know how we are acting with others and what that could possibly evoke in them. That is the only thing in the interactive process that we can really control.

Not doing this kind of work is part of the emotional fusion process in groups of people. We are all reacting to each other rather than thinking about self, getting self calm, thinking self's own thoughts, and expressing them as clearly as possible. Doing this we can step out of the group fusion process and become a stronger self. Every group will benefit when at least one person can do this.

This is part of what is involved in differentiation of self. **The better differentiated I am within an emotional system, the better chance others have to do the same.** Then we can slow down the cycle of reactivity and make better contact with one another, hopefully in a more respectful and loving way. Taking an I-position helps others to do the same. It is based on your own best thinking about the issues involved and then we can be interested in other peoples' best thinking on an issue.

Compromising, or changing one's beliefs in response to the thinking of others is just fine when it is clear this is what we are doing. It is to their credit that both James and Peter were able to change their thinking. We can defer to the principled thinking of others without buckling under to their reactivity.

As we clarify our thinking about issues, we can better choose which battles we will fight and which we will not. Dietrich Bonhoeffer's best friend and biographer, Eberhard Bethge, told about a time when they attended a Hitler rally and the huge crowd was doing their typical "Heil Hitler!" in response to his speech. Bonhoeffer joined in enthusiastically with his own "Heils." Bethge was taken aback and said, "What are you doing? We don't believe this junk." And Bonhoeffer replied, "This is nothing to die for." He didn't want to stand out in the crowd as a rebel around a mere symbol; he had more important battles to fight. We should choose our fights rather than let others choose them for us. Some things really are not worth a fight.

Differentiation or I-positions are not the same as being assertive. Assertiveness can be about what we want others to do. It can be fusion based in that we want others to join with us or go along with us in our position or belief. They can be anxiety based and evoke anxious reactivity in others. I-positions are just about what you personally will or won't do, based on your own beliefs. Period. It is understood that not everyone will believe as you do, but if you all engage in a respectful exploration of each other's beliefs, you may arrive at a new agreement. Or you may not, but there is no loss of self in the relationship fusion involved.

It is an apparent paradox that the way we change emotional systems is simply by doing a better job of defining ourselves. As we deal with the changes in life circumstances and the transitions that are thrust upon us, we can say and show where we stand and leave it to others to define where they stand. **One well-defined person in an emotional system becomes a kind of anchoring point to provide more stability for a system.** If we do something different from just reacting to others, and only manage ourselves, eventually they will stop reacting to us. They will have breathing room to think more clearly for themselves rather than reacting to pressure from us.

Differentiation and courage

I doubt very much that Paul felt very calm about going down to Jerusalem to meet with the pillars of the church and to lay before them what he was doing and what he believed. I suspect he put that visit off for a while, thinking that maybe he could avoid it. It occurred only after many years of being in his ministry, but I suspect he might have done it sooner and saved everyone a lot of grief. However, it may have taken that long for him to get his confidence and courage up.

There is a kind of groupthink that can take over a church, or any organization, as well as a family. It becomes the accepted standard of practice. **Anyone who thinks differently from the group can be up against some strong pressure to conform in beliefs and practices to the group. It takes courage to differentiate a self and not go along with the fusion of groupthink.** It takes courage to take a stand. What was it like for Martin Luther to say, "Here I stand. I can do no other." It couldn't have been easy when the Catholic Church was the only game in town and he faced certain excommunication.

Differentiation is not the same as being a rebel. Rebels simply have a problem with authority and tend to do whatever is the opposite of what authorities want in order to demonstrate to the authorities that they cannot be controlled. This is part of what the teenage years are about for teens with more authoritarian parents—and some people never lose that stance into adulthood. As adults, they have the same reactivity to authority. Rebels are not really thinking things through for self. Their thinking is still being done for them by the authorities. The rebel just does the opposite of what is wanted. This is how teens get themselves into trouble. They are not thinking about what is good for them. They are only thinking about how not to be controlled by parents or whatever authorities they are up against. This is why so many rebels end up making bad decisions for themselves.

Emotional systems do not normally welcome self-differentiating steps. Do not expect people to cheer you for taking a courageous stand. You may be seen as disturbing the peace because what they want is the togetherness of sameness. I am sure that when Paul, Barnabas, and Titus showed up in Jerusalem, many if not most of those gathered said to themselves or to one another, "Oh come on Paul, just shut up. Don't make a scene. We don't need this right now. Can't you see how difficult life is for us right now? We are being persecuted by the Romans, and condemned by the local Jews. We are losing our jobs and our income and have nothing to live on, we are poorer than we have ever been, living on the charity of others, and now you come along with these ideas of yours. You are making things worse. Let it be. We have enough trouble already."

It takes courage to maintain our beliefs and to stay in relationships with others who differ from us. Very few people back then saw Paul as the hero that we see him as today. He could have just cut off from the Jerusalem congregations and gone into the gentile world and done his own thing and leave those backward Jerusalem-based Christians alone. He could have just said to himself, "Who needs them?" and started his own denomination. However, he wanted to stay in fellowship with them. Luther didn't want to start a new church. He wanted to interact with the authorities of the church and clarify the basis of doctrine. Reactively, they kicked him out. He did not choose to leave them.

Paul had to manage his own anxiety in response to the reactivity of others to him. He had to stay calm and clear and he had to connect and be open with others. He did not hide his beliefs even though others would criticize him. This takes enormous courage. I saw this repeatedly with my clients in counseling as they began to define themselves to their partners, or to their children, or to their parents, or to other family members. They exercised great acts of courage. It is not differentiation if there is no action.

Remember the example I gave earlier of the older brother and the large ski chalet property that the family all owned together. It took tremendous courage for him to define a separate self to them, to step out of the family fusion and to say what he would and would not do, because he was going against his own long-standing emotional programming in that family, as the eldest son, to be responsible for keeping them all together and in agreement. This is what his dad had wanted. One brother called him a traitor. Another told him he was abandoning his responsibilities of keeping the family together. Especially, he was not honoring the wishes of their dead father. But later, a few months down the road, the family members begin to thank him because they also then began to feel freer from the family fusion and to think for themselves. Only much later did they praise him for making a really tough decision.

Recapping how we got here

In this session, I have been recapping my central message. Anxiety in our churches and our denomination during times of transition is a normal thing. When there is a real threat, and when our response to it is appropriate and on the mark, our anxiety can be a helpful response. It gets us moving. However, there are many more imagined threats that tend to drive us and we can spend a lot of time and energy on these and yet go nowhere with them, except to become more anxious and to spread the anxiety to others through triangulation. That is when things like some specific transition become more complicated and more difficult to get through.

As leaders in the church, we don't expect our members to be free of anxiety. We, first, just want them to be smart about it so that they can distinguish real and imagined threats. Then we want them (and ourselves) to know how to manage themselves within the anxious circumstances so they don't dump their anxiety on others and multiply its impact. Whoever can do this, will have a positive impact on the emotional system of the church, and the church will be better able to accomplish its mission in the world.

Because Paul had the courage to take on the real threat of the perversion of the gospel of freedom in Christ, and to deal directly with the church leaders involved rather than through innuendo, gossip, rumor, and triangles, or through outright hostility, the church got better focused on its message to the world.

This was Paul at his best. He was a smart man who could think clearly about theological issues and sort through the meaning of the gospel intellectually. But he was not always a calm man. In my reading of his letters, I see him sometimes being unnecessarily anxious and reactive and way too sensitive. Like us, he could lose track of being able to live the gospel. I suspect some of the problems that developed in his churches had to do with his own anxiety and sense of self, in particular his insecurity around his legitimacy as an apostle.

As leaders in a church that is based on volunteers, there are plenty of things to become anxious about. Unlike CEOs in business, we cannot just order people around, or fire the people that we consider to be a problem to our organization and who pass on their anxiety through the church. Especially in times of transition, we have to be smart in understanding whether there is a real threat, not waste our energy on imaginary threats, and find appropriate ways to address the real ones. Transition means that, of course, some things are going to have to change. This change can be threatening to some. We have to think about, where are the real threats in the transition. This requires us to be thoughtful and studious.

We don't want to become sources of anxiety ourselves, so that people feel unsafe with us, threatened by us, and further the reactivity in the church due to our behavior. People watch us and react to us. They see how we respond to threat and whether we can live the gospel in those circumstances. When we are anxious, or when we engage in triangles as a way to deal with our own anxiety, then we contribute to the anxiety in the church and help things to spin out of control.

When we are less anxious, members of the church will have a chance to catch our composure for themselves. Our steadiness becomes a source of stability for them. We don't manage them, or do this for them; we just manage ourselves as we relate to them.

Without actively relating to them, our calmness is useless. I can stay very calm when I am detached and distant from others. We have to connect with those we would rather not be around because we think they stir us up and make us anxious. First, they do not do that to us. We make ourselves anxious. When we can find a way to deal with that anxiety-creating process within us, the very same behavior in them will not lead to anxiety in us. Of course, they, in their behavior, provide an occasion for our anxiety to be stirred up, but they do not make it happen. As Sue learned to do these things, she would be able to sit comfortably with Joe, or whoever was important in her life, and work toward a common solution of the issues involved.

Looking back over my own career, I can pretty clearly see the times when I allowed my anxiety to take over. I either let myself become reactive to people and engaged in conflictual behavior with them so that things got worse, or I withdrew and distanced from them and did not connect directly with them. I distanced because I did not know how to calmly connect with them and think things through with them. Perhaps some of you can identify with that. Going back to those situations, I wish that I had the resource of Bowen theory. I could have managed myself better. Some things would have gone much better.

Here is a recent, very small example with my wife. She was feeling some stress about what she was working on. I asked a question that was easy for her to hear as a potential complaint about what was not happening. She did not want to hear any complaints at that time and so she blurted out, "I am busy here so shut up." There was a day that I could have been reactive to her "You . . . " message. But, instead, I was able to say lightly, "Ah, the pre-emptive Shut up." We chuckled together and avoided an unnecessary fight.

In the same vein, without knowing the theory but being able to enact what the theory describes, due to an innate level of differentiation that we each have some level of, I did well in circumstances that others might not have done. I attribute my successes to that, as well might you all. I describe some of my successes in the polarization book.

The rational system and the emotional system in decision-making

In the church, as in most organizations, there is a way things are supposed to be done, as outlined in our constitutions, by-laws, and rules for procedures in decision-making. That is the rational system. Then there is the emotional system we all are a part of and that often can be more powerful. If these two systems are somewhat in alignment, then usually the church functions fairly well. Life within that church is predictable, reliable, and open so that everyone understands what is going on and is relatively satisfied with it.

As anxiety begins to take over, then it often becomes a case of "the rules be damned." People act on their anxiety and disregard the rational system. Job descriptions are ignored. Policies and procedures are circumvented. Some people refuse to be responsible. It can become like guerilla warfare inside the system with each group plotting how not to let the other group be in charge or get the upper hand. When the I-position of the leaders is consistent with the rational system, and the leader can stick with it, and maintain contact with everyone involved, normally things will eventually calm down. The leader, in his or her life and actions, endorses the rational system. But, very often, the leader begins to operate more within the emotional system as well. While the leader's words say one thing, the leader's actions may say something else.

Transitional times may often involve changes in the rules and regulations of the rational system itself, like today with the ordination of gay members of the church. This is what was involved in the Jerusalem conference for those early church leaders. They were creating a new rational system; a new rationale for how their official system would function. It really was something totally new.

When leaders are working only out of their emotional system rather than the rational system, it is usually because of their own level of anxiety and their efforts to relieve it. As they get focused on winning the battle, like getting some cause of their approved, the leader may, for example, find ways to subvert normal procedures. They could, for example, offer rewards for friends, say with more money in their budget, and to punish the perceived enemies, by reducing their money or even their department.

If there is a genuine crisis in the church, then the leader's prerogative on this may be appropriate, but the action has to be open and understood by all involved for what it is. This often happens in times of transition when a new situation has emerged and the life of the organization, inevitably, is going to be changed. Budgets will change and that can stir up the emotional system.

Here is another critical ingredient in the emotional system. We all know about church leaders who are charismatic and inspiring. Very often the

church will go along with whatever that leader proposes because they value that style of leader and what it does for their church. Often the members fuse emotionally with the charismatic leader. New members come to that church because of the leader's personality. Life in the church is focused around his or her personality. And when this happens, the membership and the officers start focusing on keeping this leader happy and not contradicting him or her. This is an example of when the emotional system can begin to subvert the rational system.

A prime example of the emotional system subverting the rational system is when there is sexual abuse of church members by the leader. Very often, popular, charismatic leaders perpetrate this abuse. They have powerful personalities. When the abuse is revealed to the membership, they often deny it really happened. Or, they don't believe the victim. Or, there is a tendency for the members to say, in effect, "Well, so what, these things happen. We don't want to lose this leader who has been so valuable to us." If they believe it happened, then they may blame the victim. They say things like, "She threw herself at him. She seduced him." The victim herself will be hesitant to say anything because she knows the leader is well loved and she might be discredited or blamed. And the leader himself may rationalize his abuse as an "act of caring." Yes, really, that has been said. The emotional system takes over the church and at least some of the membership becomes reactive to the idea of removing that leader from the church. They ignore the rational procedures of the church because of their anxiety.

As churches evolve to adapt and modify its rational procedures to the actions of a charismatic leader, that church is going to run into trouble. This is just one way the emotional system begins to take over. **When there is a cult of personality around the leader, emotionality becomes a powerful force in the church.** When the cause that that leader represents becomes pervasive, the rules change and it is a completely new ball game. Even lying and deception can be rationalized. In these emotional systems not only does the cause become most important, but also the leaders and the members are super-dedicated to each other. They are fused with one another. Individuality and thinking for self is discouraged. Each is attempting to keep the other happy, and when one party fails to do that, they are blamed and told they are selling out to the other side.

When the official procedures and rules are upheld, when the rational system is followed regardless of the personality of the leader, then that church will stay sane and balanced. If irrational but popular charismatic leaders take over, who can generate and heighten peoples' anxiety about some imaginary threat, and focus peoples' anxiety on this threat, and channel it into their cause, then the emotional system will be running the church.

When things don't go as planned, eventually the reactive emotionality of the people may change the focus of the people. Then they may blame that leader for this failure. They are still anxious and now it is the leader's fault. Moses learned this while wandering the Sinai. He barely survived the people's revolt against him and his own reactivity to them and to God ended his chance of entering the Promised

Land. This dramatic situation in the Sinai is a good example of the takeover of the emotional system for the whole community.

When decisions are shaped by the personalities involved, and the politics that spring up around that person or persons, then the rational system will be subverted, and the basic principles of the church are lost and damaging conflict is inevitable. When we attempt to make decisions based on the issues involved, not on the basis of the personalities of those who represent leadership in a conflict, and when the basic principles of the church are respected, and the leaders act consistently within the established procedures, then that church will survive a crisis. It will have respect for itself, even though there will still be winners and losers on a particular issue.

When our practice fits our professed principles around a particular issue, when there is consistency between them, and when practice is not subverted by a popular personality or run by the emotionality of the system, then we can be proud of our behavior, even if we lose. Such rational behavior does not guarantee success in winning everyone over. I suppose our best example here is Jesus himself. In general, this kind of leader will normally do well in a church.

One problem we are up against in church leadership is the vast amount of leadership material, written for the business community about management that focuses on the personal qualities of good leaders. These most often have to do with personality, and not with differentiation of self. By the way, I hope you know that the CEO models that are often upheld for leadership in churches do not really work in the church. We are not a for-profit business. As a volunteer organization, we do not have leaders with the powers of a CEO. I have known personally and read about former CEOs who have decided to go into non-profit work and they quickly discover that the way they functioned in their business life does not work at all in a volunteer organization. They have to learn a completely new way of functioning if they are to succeed. They develop a new admiration for our kind of work as leaders in the voluntary organization of the church.

Whatever our style of leadership, very often the problems in a church will be related to our functioning as leaders, even if we are not directly implicated in the issues. If there is some vicious triangling going on in a church, that you think you are not a part of, think again. **Jeff Miller says:**

> Three people in a room are simply three people in a room. Three people in a room become a triangle when something is making them anxious. Most people feel anxious at some level about where they stand with the boss. So if you are in a room with two other people and you happen to be the boss, it is safe to assume that the relationship you are in is a triangle. You don't even have to be in the room.
>
> —*The Anxious Organization*, p. 199

Bringing it all together in transitions

As leaders, we are honorary members of many triangles that we don't even know about, as in the Miller quote above. That is just a fact. Members are often vying to be in the inside position with us. Their vying is evidence of the triangle with us while we are innocently going about our business. This is standard in most churches, but **the emotional process can be heightened in times of transition, when personnel changes are being made, and when all the previous alliances either are abandoned or up in the air, and new relationships are being developed**. When we come into a new leadership position in a new church, this is a primary dynamic going on and the vying becomes more intense. I am a fan of the Victorian novelist Anthony Trollope. His series of six novels called the Barchester Chronicles is full of stories about this kind of process in the church and in society generally.

You have no control over the actions or efforts of others. The only thing you can manage is yourself. Keeping self as calm as possible, avoiding any sign of favoritism in triangles, and being even-handed, following the rational procedures is the best we can do. We remain open and available to all, listening to all, while showing no interest in what one person tells you about another person who is not present, positive or negative. Certainly do not say anything negative about that person, but remain interested only in the person who is talking with you, not in their opinions about others. Do that and you are stepping right into the triangle. As you engage in detriangling self on a consistent basis, triangling within the church will decrease.

When conflicts break out between two other members and they come to you to resolve it, you still must not take sides. You define self, based on the rational principles of the church procedures and beliefs. You attempt to be a resource to each of them, with their own emotionality and thoughtfulness. It is not wrong that there are conflicts. They are normal. What will become difficult is if you join in to the triangular difficulties involved and take a side.

When blaming and scapegoating develop in a church, you have to assume you have a part in it even if you think you are not involved. Anxiety is present in the system when this happens, and you must look within. Have you been feeling some anxiety lately? How can you better manage your anxiety? You might even let others know about your anxiety and perhaps the ways you have been ignoring it or mismanaging it. This will allow others to reflect on their own anxiety and self-management.

When people start distancing from you, do what you can to maintain a connection without becoming a fierce pursuer of them. Think about what in you they may be distancing from. Send them messages that let them know you are there and interested whenever they want to reconnect with you.

Well, I could go on with practical advice. This is the place I want to end. Recognize your own anxiety and take it on, doing your best to genuinely lower it and to calm your-self so you can manage self better in the inevitable triangles. Then focus on your own beliefs and goals for how you want to be present in the church system. This is one of the best things you can do for your church, and as a leader in that church. We have rational procedures for dealing with the difficulties and conflicts that inevitably arise, and as close as we can stay to these, with our own I-positions reflecting these, while relating to all involved, we will do the best possible job as leaders in the church, especially during times of transition.

Thank you for your attention.

57900767R00058

Made in the USA
San Bernardino, CA
22 November 2017